Property;

Creating Your Dream Life With Property, Making Money Buying Property, Build Your Property Portfolio

By

Atacius Hollandbrook

All Rights Reserved. No part of this publication may be reproduced in any form or by any means, including scanning, photocopying, or otherwise without prior written permission of the copyright holder. Copyright © 2016

Terms and Conditions

LEGAL NOTICE

The Publisher has strived to be as accurate and complete as possible in the creation of this report, notwithstanding the fact that he does not warrant or represent at any time that the contents within are accurate due to the rapidly changing nature of the Internet.

While all attempts have been made to verify information provided in this publication, the Publisher assumes no responsibility for errors, omissions, or contrary interpretation of the subject matter herein. Any perceived slights of specific persons, peoples, or organizations are unintentional.

In practical advice books, like anything else in life, there are no guarantees of income made. Readers are cautioned to reply on their own judgment about their individual circumstances to act accordingly.

This book is not intended for use as a source of legal, business, accounting or financial advice. All readers are advised to seek services of competent professionals in legal, business, accounting and finance fields.

Table Of Contents

Foreword

Chapter 1: Getting Starting In Property Investing

Chapter 2: Finding Potential Property For Investment

Chapter 3: Analyzing The Property

Chapter 4: Easy Questions To Ask

Chapter 5: Buying An Investment Property

Chapter 6: Overhauling Your Property

Chapter 7: How to pay for home improvements: extra mortgage borrowing or a personal loan?

Chapter 8: Strategies In Marketing Your Property

Conclusion

Foreword

Property investing is not something to be taken lightly. Careful research and a budgetary strategy are the most important elements exercised in the area of property investing.

Let's begin the journey to discovering the secrets to buying low and selling high in real estate investing.

Chapter 1: Getting Starting In Property Investing

Synopsis

The following are some considerations that should be looked into before making the very important decision to be a property investor.

The Basics

Are you a Developer or an Investor? This might seem like a strange thing to pose at first, but many novice property entrepreneurs are not quite sure what the difference is and hence go into this being a bit of both. A Developer carries out building work to either build/convert or renovate a property with a view to selling it at a profit in as short a time as possible. An Investor is only looking to get a tenant into the property to pay rent, thus providing a regular income to the investor (who becomes landlord thereafter).

Obviously there is a lot of crossover here, it's not black or white but many shades of grey. A developer might change his/her approach after the project build stage is complete and decide to let the property to a tenant. Whereas an investor might well have to carry out some kind of building work or even build the property in order to let it. In some cases the original property is flattened and a new, superior larger building replaces it.

What to Expect from a Property Project

This bit is a bit of a reality check I'm afraid. Property development and investment is stressful, expensive and time consuming. It doesn't really work to treat it as anything other than a pure and simple business. Of course you can be creative with the property to make it more attractive, but the initial purchase is all about recouping money fast. You should definitely be in a position where you are not financially stretched before you take on your first project, because it's highly likely you will be stretched once you're underway!

Property is however extremely satisfying. It is certainly possible to develop or invest in property as a full time career; but it's good to view it as long term investment initially. Once you build up to two three properties you will streamline the process.

What Development and Investment isn't...

When starting out you will discover Property investment is not an easy way to secure an income. It takes a portfolio of quite a few properties to yield a regular income of sufficient size to live on. What happens is initially, many investors feel frustrated at the pathetic amount left after Income and Corporation tax, management fees and mortgage repayments have been subtracted. The vast majority of property investors are actually in it for the long term as I alluded to previously. The aim is to increase the property capital value over 20 years or more, not the monthly income. This is certainly something to consider before beginning the process of looking for property.

Likewise, property development is not a guaranteed way of creating substantial capital over a short period of time. It would be unrealistic to expect profits in line with those seen prior to 2007. However this does ensure that everyone entering the field is serious. Making fast profits is unlikely. However researching certain areas to purchase and you will find that places go up faster than others. For example, places on the outskirts of London that have a train station close by and are fast and easily commutable to central London will be desirable. Certainly more so than a location that doesn't have access to local transport. This is an attractive quality right off the bat and will draw people in immediately. However you may want to purchase holiday homes to rent out, in which case your strategy will be different. You will want the places that are remote and picturesque.

Decide

Deciding what type of property to invest in makes a lot of difference in how the entire buying experience plays out. Different types of properties require different types of investing practices and commitments.

There are also considerations such as property market movements, which will generally affect non landed properties much more than landed ones. This of course not only applies to the sales market but also to the rental markets too.

When considering making purchases, the investor should always include a clause in the agreement whereby there are options available and in place to nullify the contracts should the intended property to be purchased is not what it was portrayed to be.

Houses also present a better option for extensions, redesigning and remodelling possibilities and this can add value to the property. With flat, apartment and condo such exercises have restrictions and various approvals have to be sought before any work can begin.

Before committing to a purchase the buyer would also need to have a thorough inspection done on the property to ensure its justifying value. Surveying the surrounding area is also something that should be done as it will defiantly have some bearing on the property value both in the present time and in the future. For example do neighbours have any major planning in process, if so what is it. This could have a massive impact on selling of your new property a year down the line. Also look at the local crime, is it good or bad. Again your prospective tenants/buyer will do the same research as you.

Preparing the satisfactory amount of financing is also something that is important when investing in property. The end result should be favorable to the investor, otherwise the entire exercise would have been wasteful and even worse can rack up debt. This could then impact on your next venture.

Think like a Trader

You are like a trader entering into the market to buy stocks. You wouldn't stake all your equity on one big entry. Obviously you could win big but you could lose big and this would take time to recover from. You own finances need to be protected at all times.

Chapter 2: Finding Potential Property For Investment

Synopsis

As for anything worth gaining in life, planning is critical to success. There are usually many types of property options available for the discerning investor, and taking the trouble and patience to find such properties will unquestionably be well worth the effort. It is imperative however to decide what kinds of real estate investment would most suit the needs and budget of the investor before actually venturing into the actual sourcing for the ideal fit.

Testing the Waters

Once you have your intended budget set, it's time to see what's out there. Of course this is the bit most people enjoy because the process of identifying an appropriate property brings out the idealistic side in them. It is very important however, to look at it from a business point of view and more importantly already know your target market first in the specified area your looking in.

Which Market?

Many property investors specialise in a particular market because they know it well. A good example is student properties in university towns and cities. If an in-depth knowledge of the market is already there, then the approach to structuring a portfolio or renovating a property is a lot more straight-forward. It's a great idea to get a feel for the area. Chatting to estate and letting agents helps in this phase as they will be able to tell you if there is a shortfall in supply of particular property types.

It's also quite important to look at properties close to where you already live. If you are converting or renovating, this is an obvious point. However if you are an investor you might think that you can get by without needing to around the place on a day to day basis. But there will be times when you need to attend the property.

In addition, it always helps if you know the area you are investing in, as you will know if the property is selling at a decent price.

The first place to look for prospective properties is estate agents and property search websites such as Zoopla and Rightmove. A property auction is also an excellent place to look for properties, although this is one area where you will have needed to have researched the place thoroughly before bidding.

Where Is It?

There are several popular reasons as to why most investors in the property market make a particular purchase. These may include a purchase for long term rental income, for flip over profits, for long term investment and any other reasons that will contribute to some form of profit for the investor.

Once this has been decided upon then the relevant corresponding properties can be identified and purchased to suit the specific intentions of the investor.

Preparation

Preparing the finances for such investments, is also something that should be considered extensively as the form of financing used should not eventually cause the investor to be burdened with interest payments that will not make the investment viable after all.

Get your Legal side sorted

Having the expert advice of good legal counsel is also a very important service to have. Such counsel, will be able to provide information on the responsibilities of both the owner and the tenant, should the investment be for rental purposes.

Other advice can also be forthcoming through the services of legal counsel, such as the setting up of a company if the investor intends to make more purchases or investments in property. This could certainly save money for tax reasons.

Chapter 3: Analyzing The Property

Synopsis

The process of analyzing the intended returns the property is hoped to gain is done by three very different methods.

They would include:

- The gross yield
- The net yield
- Cash flow yield.

All three methods will effectively show the investor the type of returns that are likely to be enjoyed through the acquisition of the intended property.

Gross Yield

Gross yield is where the rental is calculated on a 52 week ratio and then divided by the purchase price. The figure derived from this calculation is the gross yield in percentage.

This is a fairly simple way of making a calculation to deduce if the property will present a viable return.

Net Yield

The net yield is a little more complicated as it takes into account several different factors before making a calculation on the profits it derives.

Points that are taken into consideration as reflected in the eventual calculations are such as, rates either local or regional whichever one applies, insurance costs, provisions for repairs and maintenance, vacancy periods and other expenses that might be incurred.

Therefore in this scenario the calculations would be based on the weekly rental multiplied by the on year period which is 52 weeks, whereupon the estimated expenses would be deducted from this figure and then the balance would be divided by the cost of the property. The total derived would reflect the percentage of profit yielded.

Cash Flow Yield

While the cash flow yield is also just an estimate it portrays a much clearer image of the true yields when compared to the other two types. Here the interest rates and other expenses and taxes are also included in the general calculations.

Therefore before any obligation is made, it would be advantageous to conduct any one of these analyzing tactics to ensure a wise investment is done.

Chapter 4: Easy Questions To Ask

Before putting in an offer, pose as many questions as possible - and get important answers in writing. Nothing is too silly. Even if they don't tell the truth, you may notice them squirming when you broach certain subjects. You want to build an image of the property you are purchasing. Obviously nothing will ever be perfect in every single aspect, no place ever is.

1. How many viewings has it had?
2. How many offers has it had?
3. How long has it been on the market?
4. Can I see electrical and gas installation checks/reports?
5. How long is the lease (if it has one)?
6. Have there been any neighbour disputes?
7. Why are the vendors moving and are they sure they want to sell now?
8. What renovations have been done?
9. How old is the boiler and when was it last inspected?
10. When was it last rewired?
11. Where are the vendors moving to - is there a chain?
12. If a flat, how much are service charges and ground rent? (Read more on charges.)
13. Who lives upstairs/downstairs/next door?
14. How long has the seller lived there?
15. What's included in the sale? White goods? Curtains? Wood burner?
16. Are there any parking issues?
17. If there's a real fire, is it safe to use?
18. Have there been any subsidence problems?
19. What's the council tax band? (Also check this yourself.)
20. Has anyone ever been murdered here? (Google the address too.)

You can then put together all the answers and work out the pros and cons of the place. You may even have an angle to put in a low offer.

Chapter 5: Buying An Investment Property

Synopsis

When considering the investment property platform to make money, the individual must be sure that the adequate amounts of funds are available for the purchasing process. As an income investment for those with enough money to raise a big deposit buy-to-let looks eye-catching, especially compared to low savings rates and stock market swings.

Meanwhile, the property market bouncing back has encouraged more investors to snap up property in the hope of its value rising. Mortgage rates at record lows are helping buy-to-let investors make deals stack up.

But beware low rates. One day they must rise and you need to know your investment can stand that test.

Also from what I've heard there is also a tax rise coming, as buy-to-let mortgage interest relief is axed and replaced with a 20 per cent tax credit. Additionally, from April 2016 landlords now have to pay an extra 3% stamp duty on property purchases.

Rates

Recent history provides an important lesson in how returns can be hit. Many investors who bought in the boom years before 2007 struggled as mortgage rates rose. A sizeable number were thrown a lifeline when the base rate was slashed to 0.5 per cent. Rates have stuck there since 2008, but remember they will rise again.

Yet despite the tax changes and potential for mortgage costs to rise, greater demand from tenants, rents that should rise with inflation and the long prospect for interest rate rises, mean many investors are still tempted by buy-to-let.

If you are planning on investing, or just want to know more, we tell you the ten essential things to consider for a successful buy-to-let investment.

Like any investment, buy-to-let comes with no guarantees, but for those who have more faith in bricks and mortar than stocks and shares below are This is Money's top ten tips.

Lenders have slashed rates on buy-to-let mortgages to record lows to keep the market alive as the Chancellor cracks down.

Estate agents and banks reported a last-minute rush to buy second properties before a 3 per cent stamp duty surcharge on second homes arrived on April 1 - and lenders have slashed rates to keep landlord business coming in. The average rate two-year fixed-rate buy-to-let deal has fallen to 3.32 per cent – down from 3.59 per cent last April and 5.21 per cent in April 2011. HSBC and Virgin Money have cut rates on two-year fixes to below 2 per cent.

Average rates for five-year fixed rate buy-to-let deals are at a record low of 4 per cent, according to Moneyfacts.

The buy-to-let mortgage you will be offered depends on your circumstances and the lender's criteria. Ideally, they prefer bigger deposits, strong rent to mortgage payments cover and healthy earnings elsewhere.

Purchasing

Most investment property ventures, involve having to invest and then hold on to the said property for a long term period or when the property value rises to the point where the investor is satisfied with the yield and is ready to sell.

The types of property invested in and the location where the investment is situated all play a essential role in ensuring if the investment will eventually yield the desired returns.

Unless the investor has the ready cash it would be rather unwise to invest in this form of property investment as the risks are considerably higher.

If there are insufficient funds then it is very likely that the investor would be saddled with costs instead of profits. Getting expert advice from self-regulating sources that would only have the investor's interest in mind, would help to a certain extent keep looses if any at a minimum.

Because the investment property requires a long term commitment, the investor should be prepared to calculate the cost of ownership.

These may include expenditures from owning and managing the property over a long period of time. Some of the expenses would include property taxes, insurances, utilities, maintenance, vacancies and repairs.

On the plus side there are also tax reliefs and benefits to be enjoyed in this type of investment. At the very least if the property is measured a good buy; the risks the owner is likely to face are comparatively lower than other types of investments with higher risk ratios.

Chapter 6: Overhauling Your Property

Synopsis

The overhaul exercise need not necessarily be one that incurs high costs and time. With a few adjustments the overhaul experience can be something to be thoroughly enjoyed.

Before you splash out on an extension or conservatory you should work out the costs and see how much value they will actually add to your property and whether the time and effort would be worth it.

A survey by the National Association of Estate Agents last year revealed the top home improvements that could add the best value to your property.

Half of estate agents who responded ranked adding a bedroom, usually by converting loft space as the best modification.

A third of respondents suggested a kitchen added the best value, while others suggested a conservatory or turning a garage into living space.

Similar research by estate agents and property consultancies based on those who have sold properties, shows the most valuable additions are an extra bedroom, loft conversion, bathroom, new kitchen and central heating.

Planning Consent

Ensuring the property you purchase for either development or investment holds the appropriate planning consent for what you intend to do to it. So for example if you want to convert a shop into a residential property, a farm building into flats then planning permission will be required to do this. To carry out works on a property without planning permission is illegal, and local authorities have powers to return the land or property to its original state if no consent is in place. In practice however, they often encourage retrospective planning applications so enforcement action might be unnecessary. But I certainly wouldn't recommend building anything without planning permission. Imagine you want to sell the property and you haven't got the required planning permission. Not only with a prospective buyer find out but you could be waiting months for the council/local authorities to get round to coming to a solution.

Planning rules change very often, some work that would have required permission 12 months ago might now be regarded as 'permitted development'. This means that for some building works, no planning consent is needed.

Another, extremely important aspect of planning building work is Building Regulations. In common with planning permission, building 'regs' have to be complied with by law. They are put in place to ensure that properties are renovated and built to the highest standards, and no danger exists to occupants and people in the immediate vicinity. Detailed plans have to be submitted to the local authority prior to build and follow-up inspections are also made to ensure agreement.

Build Phase

There are quite a few different ways to approach this. Many novice developers and investors carry out a high proportion of the work themselves. This is a good idea initially as it can reduce the build costs considerably. It must be balanced though with quality and time. If your experience in carrying out building work is limited, then the quality is likely to suffer.

For example if you are attempting plastering walls and ceilings for the first time then this will result in wasted time and effort to get it right. If you're happy to go through this process then why not and enjoy it. But if time is a key factor then a professional will do a far superior job in half the time. You may also need to rectify work you carried out. There is also an argument for not doing excessive work. A new purchaser could want to demolish that new kitchen you spent months renovating to an extreme standard. Everything should be of a 'very good' standard. Any higher and you are improving things on a small % basis for smaller and smaller return at a higher and higher cost. Obviously, it's a decision only the developer or investor can make and comes back to your research for the area and target market.

Building Contractors

Try where possible to use recommended contractors. Ask to speak to a previous customer. There are plenty of good builders out there despite the horror stories, however you must be careful. Always get a fixed quote. They should come round promptly and give you a specified quote for the work carried out. There can be no hidden costs. This needs to made clear. So if one builder won't cooperate, find another.

So how much would the top home improvements cost and what value would they add?

An Extension

Extensions can vary hugely, from two-storey ones that almost double a house in size to the addition of an extra downstairs room.

Because they are so varied it is difficult to put a figure on how much they cost or how much value they will add.

An extension done well that adds good-sized extra rooms in a way that is sympathetic to your home or transforms its character coherently can be a major selling point – and one you can enjoy for many years as an owner.

A Loft Conversion

Adding an extra bedroom can add around 9 to 10 per cent to the value of your home, particularly if it's a loft conversion.

It is important to not eat into living space to do it, but if there is room to expand into your loft you could get a decent return – and some much needed extra space.

Depending on the size and the location of your property, you should expect to pay £15,000/$25,000 for a small loft conversion or £25,000/$40,000 to £40,000/$65,000 for a big one.

You will need to inform your home insurer of any changes.

Extra Bathroom

An extra bathroom can be a great selling point on a property with the demand for en-suites fuelling this trend.

An extra bathroom could add 6 per cent to your property value.

Depending on the type of tiles, fixtures and fittings you want, a new bathroom could cost from £2,500/$4000 to more than £6,000/$10,000.

New kitchen

A kitchen is often the focal point of a home and can reflect the owner's tastes and personality.

It may be the first thing a buyer looks to replace, so if you can provide a ready-made, attractive space, buyers may be willing to pay more to save themselves the hassle of arranging a new kitchen. But you want to be careful how much you spend because people tend to want to put their own mark on areas like the kitchen anyway.

The big change in recent years has been the trend for open plan kitchen, dining and living spaces

A new kitchen costs on average £8,000/$14,000, but could add around 6 per cent to the value of your property.

Conservatory

A conservatory provides an extra room in your house, but means giving up some garden space. If it is under a certain size, you won't need planning permission and could do it under permitted development

A conservatory can be a good way of delivering extra space for less or getting some open plan living, especially if it's enlarging for example a small kitchen or a cramped living room. You may have to abide by rules on doors closing off areas.

Your conservatory could boost your property value by 5 per cent, but expect to pay between £4,000/$6000 and £10,000/$18,000.

The following are some tips to follow in the quest to overhaul the property and yet bust the bank.

Theme

Trying to have some sort of theme in mind, so that there can be some standardized use of material would be very helpful. If the main material is bought in bulk it would be much cheaper and the individual can then apply some level of creatively to each area, to still keep it looking somewhat individualistic in style. For example giving the place a more rustic feel, changing the doors to an old wooden look, matching the skirting boards etc

De-clutter

Conducting a de cluttering exercise maybe all that is needed to create a new look. This style of overhauling will not only be cheaper, but it can also be surprising different, when the eventual look of the room becomes unrecognizable from its original state. Getting rid of everything and then starting out with just the bare necessities from the lot is a good place to start.

Colour

This ties in with theme and adding a reoccurring colour can be a simple and subtle way of tying in the house design without breaking the bank. Adding a little color or changing an existing loud color for something more sedate and tranquil will effectively create a new and calmly inviting atmosphere. Very light colours can make a room feel more airy and spacious. This is also another cheap way of conducting an overhaul. There is even the popular use of motifs to consider when making choices for the overhaul exercise.

Furniture

Obviously if you're selling the house then you will take furniture with you, letting will be negotiable. But changing out some old chairs in a kitchen for stylish bar stalls for example is a simple change that may lend to an overall style you're creating. Perhaps you're going for a rustic look and all the furniture is very modern. Changing a few pieces of furniture for effect that you could source from a jumble sale is a great idea. From bedrooms to kitchens new furniture and fixtures can do wonder toward creating a new look.

Other larger and more important task that may need serious attention during the overhaul exercise would be the plumbing and wiring of the property. This should be addressed, especially if the property is rather old.

Chapter 7: How to pay for home improvements: extra mortgage borrowing or a personal loan?

Improvements can rack up costs if the property needs a lot of work. If you don't have enough put away or don't want to use your savings, extra mortgage borrowing or a personal loan are the most common options.

Both mortgage and personal loan rates have fallen to record lows (in the UK), but you need to compare all costs including fees so you know exactly how much you will be reimbursing.

Personal loans typically last between one, three or five years at a set rate, whereas a mortgage is usually for around 25 years with a set deal period at first before moving to a higher standard variable rate.

Additional mortgage borrowing is typically done over the remaining lifetime of your existing mortgage.

The advantage with raising the funds through mortgage is that you will usually be able to borrow a larger amount and pay a lower interest rate as the loan is secured on your home.

You can take out supplementary borrowing against your home with your mortgage lender providing you have enough equity to do so – and remain below your bank or building society's maximum loan-to-value levels for mortgages.

This will typically done either on one of the fixed, tracker or variable rate deals they currently offer for additional borrowing and will sit alongside your existing mortgage. That is likely to mean that you may have two parts of your mortgage on different rates. There can be early reimbursement charges if you want to pay it back early.

You will need to be assessed, however, on tougher affordability rules that came into effect last year. This can make the process take its time and you may need to supply a lot of information and paperwork.

Personal Loan

Personal loan rates have fallen to record low levels, with some below 4 per cent. The advantage of a personal loan is that you can usually borrow up to £25,000 on an unsecured loan and get a quicker decision. A personal loan is unsecured and so your home is not at risk if you default.

The borrowing process is also less invasive and time consuming. While the rate on a personal loan may be higher, you could rack up less interest overall as you're paying the money back over a much shorter period.

It is important to remember that any mortgage or additional borrowing will be secured against your home, if you fail to meet repayments you could end up losing the property.

The application process for a loan is considerably easier and quicker than a mortgage, as you can usually do it online.

A mortgage application can take months while a loan decision can often be given in minutes online or on the phone. The amount and rate you actually get is based on your credit rating.

You can usually borrow anything from £1,000 to £25,000, but the length of the loan will be shorter than a mortgage, meaning you have to pay it back quicker.

That raises monthly payments but reduces overall interest charges.

Bottom Line

If you borrowed £10,000 over five years on a 4 per cent personal loan it would carry monthly payments of £184 per month and cost you £1,050 in interest.

The same amount over 25 years on a 2.5 per cent mortgage would add just £44 to monthly payments, but cost you £3,460 in interest – more than three times as much.

You can settle a personal loan quicker by overpaying, but some providers will charge for this.

Borrowing more on your mortgage

If you have enough equity in your own home, your bank or building society could let you borrow extra money against the value of your home.

This could be done with a complete re-mortgage for the full amount but for home enhancements people usually take on additional borrowing – an extra chunk of mortgage against their home, as explained above.

Mortgage rates have fallen to record lows in recent months and you can now get a five-year fix below 2.5 per cent provided you have substantial equity of about 40 per cent.

Further down the scale, those with 10 per cent equity could fix at less than 4 per cent.

Your lender may offer you further borrowing at one of its main fixed, tracker or variable rates, or it may have special rates for additional borrowing.

This can mean that you need to take on extra borrowing at a different rate to your existing mortgage.

If you want to remortgage for the entire quantity and are still in a fixed or tracker rate deal period, check any early repayment charges with your existing lender, these could be significant.

You will also have to go through a new submission process and ensure you can comply with tougher new affordability rules introduced since April 2014.

In terms of monthly payments a mortgage will work out cheaper but the added fees on the best rates and the longer application process may not prove worthwhile if you're looking to borrow smaller amounts up to £25,000.

Chapter 8: Strategies In Marketing Your Property

Synopsis

There are several ways to create interest in the property on the market to ensure enough distinguishability to lock in a sale. The more interest the property attracts, the better the chances of it being sold or rented in a short span of time.

Today's world is full of marketing and advertising outlets and most of them are perpetually evolving - the internet, social media etc. The way your home is marketed will have a deep impact on its final sale price, so you should discuss your marketing plan in detail with your real estate agent.

The goal when marketing your home is to gain as much exposure in the market as possible to the right target audience. Increased exposure in the housing market will put your home in front of the greatest number of potential buyers. The larger your pool of buyers, the higher the likelihood you will field multiple offers.

Once you receive multiple offers the ball is firmly in your court where prospective buyers will offer their highest and best price in order to compete with other offers. This generates a buzz that your property is certainly worth purchasing because it has an added value of being 'wanted' by others. Therefore the immediate thought is that when they want to sell this place it will generate the same buzz.

The most effective strategy is to run a promotional blitz as soon as your home hits the market. Tools that your agent should incorporate in this marketing blitz include (but may not be limited to:

• Printed materials such as flyers, pamphlets, postcards, etc. that buyers can take home - be sure to include photos and list major selling points.

- Listing on the Multiple Listing Service (MLS) complete with all descriptive details

- Professional quality photographs and/or virtual tour of your home on the Internet

- Featured listing on numerous websites such as Zillow, and your agency's company website and the list of potential sites is quite long.

- Post the listing on social media sites like Facebook, Twitter, and Pinterest

- An "Agent Tour" the first week on the market

- Newspaper and/or trade magazine ads

Video

This is a new way to sell a house, and it's not what you think. Video to sell houses isn't new, it's already being done. However the new style is not to sell you the number of bedrooms and the size of the kitchen. It's to sell you the lifestyle of owning the property. What you'll do there, where you'll spend most of your time, the surrounding area, the walks in the garden, relaxing by the pool, chatting with friends in the kitchen. The locality to the train station. It's the 'why' you would live there.

If done properly, these marketing techniques can unleash a great deal of power and help to propel your listing above the competition. And while your agent is responsible for creating the lion's share of these items, the key to their effectiveness is your commitment to having your home properly staged. Photos and video virtual tours should only be taken once your house is in pristine condition. You need everything to be perfect when you invite a group of agent's to tour your home. Staging is of critical significance for both the interior and exterior of your home. If you stage your property well, you will make a good first impression – and there is nothing more valuable when trying to sell your home.

One final element to a successful marketing strategy is scrutiny. It is imperative that your agent tracks and analyzes all of your showing activity.

Great Info

The following are some strategies that can be employed in order to create this visibility and attraction:

Making a list of all the special feature that make the property stand out or be changed from others around, should be done. Included in this list should be elements that would be an attractive selling point and also hard to resists. Highlighting negative elements that definitely don't exist in this property will also portray to the prospective client, what they can avoid and thus benefit by committing to a deal on the property.

Once the list is drawn up, then the target audience attention should be actively sought and the points should be extensively publicized to ensure the desired impact of curiosity and interests are firmly established. Using captions that would personally impact and play on the prospective client's perceptions and ideals would be beneficial. Remember it's the 'why' someone would want to move there.

Talking to anybody and everybody would also help to create the free publicity for the advertising of the said property. This has been known to be an effective way of getting the required attention that eventually brings forth a successful sale.

If time and energy permits, having an open house or garage sale will also be another effective way to get the attention of interested parties. This is an ideal way of informing everyone in the area about the property being available for sale or rent depending on the owner's necessities. People attending the garage sale can also act as advertising instruments to spread the word about the availability of the property.

Conclusion

So we have finally reached the end of my book on property investing and developing. The crucial element of any business venture is to have a clear plan, establish your target audience.

So please review my book and I wish you ever success.

All the best,

Atacius

www.ingramcontent.com/pod-product-compliance
Lightning Source LLC
Chambersburg PA
CBHW071833200526
45169CB00018B/1458